my dream speech

a Choreopoem

Leslie N. Polk

Copyright @ 2012 by Leslie N. Polk

All rights reserved. No part of this publication may be reproduced, distributed, or transmitted in any form or by any means without the written permission of the author.

ISBN 978-0-615-78284-3

Unless otherwise indicated, Bible quotations are taken from New International Version of the Bible. Copyright © 1973, 1978, 1984 by International Bible Society. Zondervan Publishing House.

For Isaiah

and Uncle Jerry

My Inspiration

"I have a dream today... I have a dream that one day every valley shall be exalted, every hill and mountain shall be made low. The rough places will be made plain, and crooked places will be made straight. And the glory of the Lord shall be revealed, and all flesh shall see it together. This is our hope. This is the faith I go back to the South with. With this faith we will be able to hew out of the mountain of despair a stone of hope. With this faith we will be able to transform the jangling discourses of our nation into a beautiful symphony of brotherhood. With this faith we will be able to work together, to pray together, to struggle together, to go to jail together, to stand up for freedom together, knowing that we will be free one day."

excerpt from Dr. Martin Luther King Jr.

I Have a Dream Speech, 1963

To my mother, I love you and thank God for your patience.

To my father, I love you and I'll always be your baby girl.

To my brother, I love you and thank you for always supporting me.

To the rest of my family, the Williams and Polk, and the Hill family whom I have always known as family, I love and adore you all.

To each one of my friends: Eugene Crosier plus one (V.P, F.S, S.S, E.W); Og. 5 (sisters); 7th Street North East/DC/Howard family; my home church pastor, Reverend Kenneth Jones Jr. and Como, I love you and thank you all for your love and encouragement.

Colors of the Rainbow

Red- blood and atonement

Orange- relationship/companionship with God; Holy Spirit; intercession

Yellow- celebration and joy

Green- new life; growth

Blue- Heavenly grace

Purple- royalty and wealth

Character Synopsis

Monologue 1- park setting; older lady in shabby, green clothes, pushing a buggy; younger lady with jeans, white tee shirt, a cap, and green apron

Monologue 2- older lady in red; going back and forth from the kitchen stove to sitting in rocking chair knitting and reading.

Monologue 3- two females; young adult and child dressed in purple

Monologue 4-lady dressed in business attire with orange accents; carrying briefcase and talking on the phone

Monologue 5- lady dressed in yellow African attire; picking food and preparing meal

Monologue 6- lady dressed in casual white dress with blue accents; sitting in the church pew praying aloud

my dream speech

Grace and peace to you from God our Father and the Lord Jesus Christ. Praise be to the God and Father of our Lord Jesus Christ, who blessed us in heavenly realms with every spiritual blessing in Christ. For he chose us in him before the creation of the world to be holy and blameless in His sight. In love he predestined us for adoption to sonship through Jesus Christ, in accordance with his pleasure and will to the praise of his glorious grace, which he has freely given us in the One he loves. In him we have redemption through his blood, the forgiveness of sins, in accordance with the riches of God's grace that he lavished on us. With all wisdom and understanding, he made known to us the mystery of his will according to his good pleasure, which he purposed in Christ, to be put into effect when the times reach their fulfillment-to bring unity to all things in heaven and on earth under Christ.

Ephesians 1:2-10 NIV

GREEN

Here there is no Greek or Jew, circumcised or uncircumcised, barbarian, Scythian, slave or free, but Christ is all, and is all.

Colossians 2:11 NIV

i was walking

it started raining

Left hand:

loaves of someone's first meal since 2009

when he went from being our nation's veteran to the streets soldier

but let's take it back

how do I have a job but can't afford to get to and from there

i worked the late shift

she been acting funny

or maybe I'm just tripping

but I dare not call her

    "Hey missy."

three steps before I whisper to myself

    "Don't make eye contact."

four steps after engaging into this man's eye

    "Um hey, how you doing?"

    "Oh well I'm not gon' complain. What's in your bag?"

    "Some bread. You want some?"

    "Of course! If only you knew…"

"I'm telling you that's the story he gave me so I don't understand why we throw this stuff away. All these people out here…"

this building was standing as tall as the 20 plus feet taller buildings of DuPont Circle, that's why they forgot about them people right there

probably three days before I met **_Giorgio_**

i walked

again

occupying my time this time

with Occupy DC

Occupy the Hood

and Occupy Franklin-

a school that was shut down

later became a homeless shelter

and then was shut down

so now these people are across the street in Franklin Park with their nights view of the White House from a

cracked

wooden

bench

"So you tell me how do you first shut down one of the only supposed opportunities in your system and then the only home we know of?

we didn't go off to college
dropped out of high school
barely made it to junior high
because from day one you weren't concerned with investing
your time into our betterment
so now your betterment
becomes a false betterment
cause there I was signing up for your military
and here I am having fought with your military
and once again I am a soldier for these streets just like I was
when you decided to shut down my first opportunity."

but God gives us
the greatest and ultimate opportunity
if we just believe

Right Hand:

falling in love with Jesus

will be the best thing you've ever done if you haven't tried Him

i mean fully committed to Him

because I'd been fully committed to sin

believing I was saved because I believed in our Savior

so I thank God for the blood that covers me

cause I was failing to remember

that He as our Master

would like us to live

"as drum majors for justice peace and righteousness"

three miles from his dream speech

became a wake-up call

to *my dream speech*

everything came to be what seemed to be as nothing

all in the matter of seconds

both times

but this time

that proceeds my next line

was far different than that which I spoke of in the last nine lines

raging behind bars

which became the feeling I'd been feeling ever since I could remember

because **Giorgio's** false betterment

was just like the false freedom that's been presented

and now I've experienced the chains of those before us

the dragging

the beating

all to believe I was so angry that the thought of being in there now

for murder

didn't even matter

the markings on my body fit right in with the stories of the mates

who shared the same stories of drunken nights, high times, and lustful encounters

but Peter tells us to endure patiently just as Christ did

even in the cruelest times Jesus did no wrong

so as believers we must try to live as He did

we must all come together

because at first the man was sent to show us the ultimate opportunity

but greed and power has led to this system

which seems only to seek to kill our opportunity

to America's dream

far different than

Isaiah

Paul

or Martin Luther King Jr.'s dream

far different than

Giorgio's

and my own dream

When Christ entered the world, race, creed, and color was erased. Paul tells the Church of Colosse that Christ is all that there is to know and be like. Those who believe are now identified by faith in Christ, belonging to God as His children.

Giorgio

RED/CRIMSON

and be found in Him, not having a righteousness of my own that comes from the law, but that which is through faith in Christ- the righteousness that comes from God on the basis of faith.

Philippians 3:9

Thank God for the Holy Spirit that can move through you

understanding the difference between it

and the nonsense

if you think about it too hard

you lose the first concept

thank God for the Holy Spirit that can move through you

if you are in a constant presence with it

what a joy it could be

because even in those hard times

you'll come to remember

that it is He who has all power

as God the Father

who sent His son Christ Jesus

to save you from your sins

and because of His death

you can now be born again with the promise of life eternal

if you just believe

at times you may find yourself wallowing in

your guilt

your pain

your ailments

and worries

that you lose sight on Him who has all power

the One who can help you to live holy

yet remember we all fall

but Christ's precious blood

covers you

and grants you salvation

if you just believe in Him

My Best Friend Lindsay

Forgive me Father

for I know my hearts desires aren't as important as my spiritual needs

which can fulfill my life

with or without that which I desire

realizing experience in God comes through the Holy Spirit

that's why I must desire to be more like Him

I thank God for the Holy Spirit that works through me

 can't get more like Christ on my own

cause my own is so filled with

thoughts

pleasures

actions

and desires of worldly things

the tangible

the material

that which was created by man

Pecola

Just be still

for approved workman are not ashamed

So thank God for the Holy Spirit that works through us

for the Bible tells us

all have sinned and fall short of the glory of God

so let's thank God

that by His grace we are saved through faith

not of ourselves

but as a gift from God

so let no man boast

as if we could have done it ourselves

oh the many distractions that come our way when we try to do it ourselves

we must turn away from evil and sinful pleasures

Allowing the Spirit to work through us

through praise and worship

not only to song or dance

but to the feeling we'd get as if we were alone with the Spirit

Thank God for the Holy Spirit that works through us

Mbodze Yusef

Going back and forth

and back and forth

between what you think is wright

and what you know is wrong

or what you know is right

and what you know is wrong

forcing yourself to believe in something you cannot sensitize

have faith in your senses that He will work through them to show you just who He is

showing you it's okay to spend your time in His time

allowing you to realize it's okay to rid of any distractions

when you realize it's His time any way

Ontario…Canada that is

Cause I'm trying to travel

in His word

through His Kingdom

right here on earth

spreading the Gospel

Africa

South America

Italy

Japan

Australia

The Westside

South Dallas

5th Ward

The N.O

Mississippi

ATL

Seattle

everywhere has somewhere

where there's poor in health

poor in physicality

poor in morality

poor in spirituality

so I'm trying to travel

in His word

through His Kingdom

right here on earth

spreading the Good News

Praising God our Father

for sending His son Christ Jesus

who saves me from my iniquities

and lives through me in Spirit

so that I might reach out to be more like Him

Giorgio and Cheri'

Just believe in it

it could happen

don't be scared of it

fear the wrath of God from lacking such faith in it

fear the wrath of God for forgetting it was He who gave it

as believers we must be obedient

to the word of God

which will last forever

just like our salvation

So why not believe in the Holy Spirit to work through us

Nina, jinalangu Leslie

Afraid of everything

yet afraid of nothing

all in the same breadth

B-R-E-A-D-T-H

trying to explain to self

is leading to failure in remembering

that our wants and desires aren't as important as our needs but more importantly the needs of others

take self out of self

imagine you're standing at the top of the National Monument

or out in the middle of the Indian Ocean

Imagine allowing the Spirit to move through you

in a home all alone

with people around you

or a place where souls have connected to the Highest Majesty

or in Frederick Douglass Hall anticipating the next word that will bring light needed for a

withering

loose peddled

Chrysanthemum

Whatever work you do

Whatever gift you pursue

Praise God for the Holy Spirit to move through you

Righteousness comes through faith in Christ. Because of His saving grace, as believers we are granted the Holy Spirit. Often times we put too much confidence in flesh, believing that we can do and figure things out for ourselves. It is then that we block the Spirit and ultimately God from doing whatever work it is He desires to do for us and in us.

Rose

PURPLE

I have set my rainbow in the clouds, and it will be the sign of the covenant between me and the earth.

Genesis 9:13 NIV

Nina Simone's "Four Women" plays in my head

Aunt Sarah

Saffronia

Sweet Thing

Peaches

The four little girls at 16th Street Baptist Church bombing plays in my head

Addie Mae Collins

Cynthia Wesley

Carole Robertson

Denise McNair

Fighting the same fight

i've seen fought in my mother

who gave me the fight every time she told me she loved me

every time she tells me she loves me

which got me through the tough times when she wasn't there to tell me she loves me

who showed me that no greater love

is that of the love that comes from God our Father

who's always there because He loves me

showing His love as my *Best Friend*

also through my *Best Friend*

who shares the same name

as my childhood friend Lindsay

who makes me want to give such love

that travels to a place so pure

cause no greater love is that of a love so pure

that comes from God

our Lord and our Savior

who showed up like no other

when I became a thinker and no longer just a writer

who revealed such things long before I was a toddler

and I thank Him

for the talks

when at times I thought I was crazy

and I thank Him

when I saw the rainbow and believed in a new beginning

given the name Mbodze from the people of this cultures beginning

having to believe in God's calling

just as I believe in the light He sent to this world

who brings light to many who are like

the "Four Women"

and the four little girls

and my mother

and even to the men out there

the Mother Earth is from God our Father

so it is our duty to be lights for His Kingdom

cause I remember needing light like Chrysanthemum in Mrs. Nelson's 2nd grade class

who was similar to the colored girls who considered suicide when the rainbow was enuf

or similar to the little black girl named

Pecola

When God flooded the Earth, He sent the rainbow as a covenant to Noah that He would not destroy the earth with water again. In this covenant was also God's unfailing love with the promise of the Messiah, who came to save the world from sin.

Pecola

ORANGE

Know that a man is not justified by observing the law, but by faith in Jesus Christ. So we, too, have put our faith in Christ Jesus that we may be justified by faith in Christ and not by observing the law, because by observing the law no one will be justified.

Galatians 2:16 NIV

people ask all the time the difference between here and there

it's the same difference between me and here

and me and **Ontario**

Canada that is

it was like good and evil

here there is good and evil

there, there is good and evil

me i have good and evil

she who had good and evil

Ontario

Canada that is

sometimes i hate going back there because it brings back evil memories that make me forget all the good memories i made there

Ontario

Canada that is

the beautiful

the rich history

and culture

that was founded the same year of the place i came in contact with

Ontario

Canada that is

pondering; going back.

3…2…1…

Ring

Ring

Ring

3 rings and i restlessly answer the phone

7 syllables and i anxiously question the other end

10 seconds pass

which added to the equation of my life changes

hear me well

hear me well

what lied before me i did not know

something just told me to get up and go

1 flight

2 flight open

1 step 2 step open

3…2…1…

initial reaction

sensible reaction

both led to what i think of as God trying to get my attention but you see i did not pay attention

and im sure

im not sure of where i got lost

but in the midst of it

somebody had been praying

so i started praying

In the Name of Jesus

everything will be alright

but let's go back

cause remember i thought i got lost

but as a believer i've learned that i just fell off

cause that was probably the last time i really started praying til' adversity hit me again

you mean to tell me 2 out of 30 something g's

blood on my fingers

trying to live up to everybody else's expectations

or wait

are they my own and i'm just fearful so i put them on everybody else

man forget this
i'm done with this
i've had enuf of this

aint nothing like going through this

for let's say 18 years of what i can remember of this

trying to release of something for that long

whether it started at age 4 or 13

it's become my bad habit

but it's time to allow God to have that full attention

cause that which you desire could be that and/or much greater

i'm just speaking from experience

and reference

and now a child of God

trying to be more like His Son Christ Jesus

our Lord and Our Savior

in this journey know

Jesus has already come to save the world

so let's take the movement and the word

to try to live up to what God has first called us

to worship Him in all that we do

and because of His salvation

we as believers experience

Life after death

Heaven

not quite Thugz Mansion

but a place for a born again G

with the Almighty G

living each day for a future so
Beautiful
Beautiful
Beautiful

it takes
commitment
commitment
commitment

but it's
possible
possible
possible

In the name of Jesus
Amen

Amen and

Amen

As a believer we are promised salvation, thus we'll never be lost from God's sight. We may lose our way at times and fall to the ways of the world, but if we believe in our hearts that God sent His Son to die for our sins, we are saved.

Ontario

YELLOW

The ransomed of the Lord will return. They will enter Zion with singing; everlasting joy will crown their heads. Gladness and joy will overtake them, and sorrow and sighing will flee away.

Isaiah 51:11

LET'S GO

WOW

i've never seen anything like it

i've never felt anything like it

oh wait, it's similar to…

nah

i couldn't have dreamt anything like this

a place

so

Beautiful

Beautiful

Beautiful

it was still

but ooh the movement that surrounded us

three flies nibbled at my big toe

we could hear the cats squirming behind us

saw the family of bats flying above us

could smell the salt from the ocean as it waved on by us

and there was a bittersweet taste in knowing that it would all soon end for us

a place

so

Beautiful

Beautiful

Beautiful

Listen:

Yusef went on about life and what it meant for them

shackled buildings standing 20 plus feet high

mudded homes right next door

dirt roads paved roads dirt roads

water

dirt roads paved roads dirt roads

water

alley way public street alley way

water

alley way public street alley way

water

children mothers people

begging

bargaining shysters hustling

making a living

Massai Muslim Mombasa

culture

tribe religion people

roots

life and what it was for them?

LOOK

WOW

WHATS THAT

GET IT GET IT GET IT

allowing him to eat from my palm with his large tongue as his gold body with brown spots glistened in my view

no taller than two feet now hunched over trying to attack for the chips

families making acquaintances told by the shaking of their trunks

pregnant belly thirsting for water which caused our van to stop as her tail wagged on to meet her king…the king of the jungle

a place so

Beautiful

Beautiful

Beautiful

hungry starving swollen

mis-educated

poor wealthy

mind body soul

diseased pained

miracles

joyful aware

famine

that's why i want to go to your land

LET'S GO

WOW

i've never seen anything like it

i've never felt anything like it

skyscrapers cars

luxury

entertainment

fame money

FREEDOM

speech

religion

sexuality

ANYTHING

YET NOTHING!

its leads to nothing

free will to do good works keeps us at something

believing in Christ has to be our everything

hoods ghettos slums

poor wealthy rich

starving homeless

weak

you, could face this too

mis-educated re-educated

all to proclaim the Gospel so that we can all see a place so

Beautiful

Beautiful

Beautiful

i got to make it to His Land

cause at times we want theirs

and they long for ours

but when Jesus returns

for believers it will ALL be well

The Heaven and earth we know of now will be no more when Jesus returns. For believers this is a Beautiful thing. No more pain and sorrow, but praise and worship for the God our Father.

Yusef

BLUE

If I have the gift of prophecy and can fathom all mysteries and all knowledge, and if I have faith that can move mountains, but have not love, I am nothing.

1 Corinthians 13:2 NIV

Best Friend,

We've met before

and it was times I hated you then

erosion felt at the pit of my stomach as i break down the very thought of you and why you keep coming back

my skin crawls

my throat dries

my lungs tighten

causing my ribs to puncture my soul

because i cannot fathom the fact that you are still here

you make my head spin

my fingers

and my toes tight

We've met before

Travel with me to a place so pure

cause no greater love is that of a love so pure

pure as a virgin's unpopped cherry

you see like her

my love awaits that journey

where souls meet body

two become one body

and not just with anybody

our conscious must connect

linking our spirits to the Highest Majesty

We've met before

falling in love with Jesus

is the best thing you could ever do

if you haven't tried Him

because there are times when God should feel as though

He should hate our every part of being

but He has a love so pure

through faith in His Son

and the Spirit

which will lead us to the Highest Majesty

We've met before

i've seen it

i've experienced it

all with you before

it would go something just like this

but this time you're not leaving

because i believe in it

i am your virgin

i submit to you

the way you respect me

man and woman

as one in Christ

my husband

your wife

We've met before

past that would not allow me to believe in future

future already destined from the past

we give Him our hearts desires

and He lays out the steps

never said it would be easy

but oh the things you gain

living in pure love through Christ Jesus

with our Father

i think you should meet Him

or re meet Him

whichever it may be

Without the love of God we are nothing. Our lives lead to nothing. As believers we have the gift of God's love through Christ Jesus, who came to give us life more abundantly. When we make mistakes and commit sin we can always come back to Him with a Spirit of repentance and the desire to submit to His will in not continuing to make the same mistakes. Marriage is a sacred covenant which was made to exhibit how to live out God's love. Man and woman as one in Christ, who then helps to lead the couple in raising children to execute God's love in an upright way.

Best Friend

Notes

Page	Notes

Green

2	**Colossians 2:11 Here there is no...** When Christ entered the world, race, creed, color, etc was erased. Paul tells the church of Colosse that Christ is all that there is to know and be like. Those who believe are now identified by faith in Christ, belonging to God as His children.
5	**DuPont Circle** is a historic district in Northwest Washington, DC
5	The Occupy movement was an international protest movement against social and economic inequality. **Occupy D.C.** was an occupation of public space in Washington, D.C., based at McPherson Square. **Occupy the Hood** was a sub-movement that started in New York and Detroit and had spread to other cities, including D.C., by Oct 2011. **Occupy Franklin School** was a sub movement of Occupy DC for an abandoned school and most recent at the time, a homeless shelter.
6	Martin Luther King Jr., 1968 sermon at Ebenezer Baptist Church in Atlanta. "If you want to say that I was a drum major, say that I was a drum major for justice. Say that I was a drum major for peace. I was a drum major for righteousness. And all of the other shallow things will not matter." The Old Testament explains justice and righteousness to be one in the same which grants peace. Something wholly only achieved by God, who is the only one with the right to judge the unjust and unrighteous. Whose mercy is far greater than justice.
7	Martin Luther King Jr., "I Have a Dream Speech," August 28, 1963, Washington DC Civil Rights March.

8   1 Peter 2:21-23 (NIV)
To this you were called, because Christ suffered for you, leaving you an example, that you should follow in His steps. "He committed no sin, and no deceit was found in His mouth." When they hurled their insults, He did not retaliate…

RED (Crimson)

10   **Philippians 3:9 and be found…basis of faith**
Righteousness comes through faith in Christ. Because of His saving grace, as believers we are granted the Holy Spirit. Often times we put too much confidence in flesh, believing that we can do and figure things out for ourselves. It is then that we block the Spirit and ultimately God from doing whatever work it is He desires to do for us and in us.

14   2 Timothy 2:15 (NIV)
Do your best to present yourself to God as one approved, a workman who does not need to be ashamed and who correctly handles the word of truth.

14   Romans 3:23 (NIV)
For all have sinned and fall short of the glory of God.

14   Ephesians 2:8-9 (NIV)
For it is by faith you are save and this is not from yourselves, it is the gift of God; not by works, so that no one can boast.

18   **The Frederick Douglass Memorial Hall** (1935) is named in honor of Frederick Douglass, the revered abolitionist and past trustee and participant of Howard University (1867).

18   1 Corinthians 10:31
            So whether you eat or drink or whatever you do, do it all for the glory of God.

PURPLE

22   **Genesis 9:13 I have set…me and the earth**
            When God flooded the Earth, He sent the rainbow as a covenant to Noah that He would not destroy the earth with water again but with fire. In this covenant also lies God's unfailing love with the promise of the Messiah, who came to save the world from their sins. Thus, when the Lord returns with fire those who believe will be caught up with Him and not in the rapture.

23   Nina Simone. "Four Women." *Wild Is the Wind*. Philips Records, 1966. Vinyl recording

23   **16th Street Baptist Church Bombing,** located in Birmingham, Alabama; African American church bombed in 1963 as an act of racial terrorism, killing four little girls in the basement.

24   **Mbodze**, mother of the first nine Mjikenda tribes of east Africa.

25   **Chrysanthemum**, main character: Henkes, Kevin. *Chrysanthemum*. New York: Mulberry, 1991. Print

25   Shange, Ntzoke. *For Colored Girls Who Have Considered Suicide When the Rainbow was Enuf: a chore poem*. The University of Michigan, 1974. Print.

25   **Pecola**, main character: Morrison, Toni. *The Bluest Eye*. Holt, Rinehart, and Winston, 1970. Print

ORANGE

27   **Galatians 2:16 Know that…no one will be justified**
As a believer we are promised salvation, thus we'll never be lost from God's sight. We may lose our way at times and fall to the ways of the world, but if we believe in our hearts that God sent His Son to die for our sins, we are saved.

28   **Ontario**, province of Canada; located in east-central Canada; founded in 1867

32   Tupac. "Thugz Mansion." *Better Dayz*. Amaru, 2002. CD

YELLOW

34   **Isaiah 51:11 The ransomed…flee away**
The Heaven and earth we know of now will be no more when Jesus returns. For believers this is a Beautiful thing. No more pain and sorrow, but praise and worship for God our Father.

36   **Maasai**, semi-nomadic people located in Kenya and northern Tanzania

36   **Muslim**, believers of the monotheistic Islamic faith; followers of the Qu'ran which they consider to be God's word to the prophet Muhammad.

36   **Mombasa**, the second largest city in Kenya, Africa.

BLUE

43   **1 Corinthians 13:2 If I have… I am nothing**
Without the love of God we are nothing. Our lives lead to nothing. As believers we have the gift of God's love through Christ Jesus, and when we make mistakes

and commit sin we can always come back to Him with a Spirit of repentance. Marriage is a sacred covenant which was made to exhibit how to live out God's love. Man and woman as one in Christ, who then helps to lead the couple in raising children to execute God's love in an upright way.

Scripture References

I am not saying this because I am need, for I have learned how to be content whatever the circumstances. I know what it is to be in need, and I know what it is to have plenty. I have learned the secret of being content in any and every situation, whether well fed or hungry, whether living in plenty or in want. I can do everything through him who gives me strength.

Philippians 4:11-13

The King will reply, I tell you the truth, whatever you did for one of the least of these brothers of mine, you did for me.

Matthew 25:40

The man of integrity walks securely, but he who takes crooked paths will be found out.

Proverbs 10:9

Dear friends, let us love one another, for love comes from God. Everyone who loves has been born of God and knows God.

1 John 4:7

We know that we live in Him and He in us, because He has given us of His Spirit.

1 John 4:13

Do not be anxious about anything, but in everything, by prayer and petition, with thanksgiving, present your requests to God. And the peace of God, which transcends all understanding, will guard your hearts and your minds in Christ Jesus.

Philippians 4:6-7

For God did not give us a spirit of timidity, but a spirit of power, of love and self-discipline.

2 Timothy 1:7

But He was pierced for our transgressions, He was crushed for our iniquities; the punishment that bought us peace was upon Him, and by His wounds we are healed.

Isaiah 53:4-5

Likewise, teach the older women to be reverent in the way they live, not to be slanderers or addicted to much wine, but to teach what is good. Then they can train the younger women to love their husbands and their children, to be self-controlled and pure…so that no one will malign the word of God.

Titus 2:3-5

I have been crucified with Christ and I no longer live but Christ lives in me. The life I live in the body, I live by faith in the Son of God, who loved me, and gave himself for me.

Galatians 2:20

How great is the love the Father has lavished on us, that we shall be called children of God! And that is what we are! The reason that the world does not know us is that it did not know him.

1 John 3:1

Even though I walk through the valley of the shadow of death, I will fear no evil, for you are with me, your rod and staff, they comfort me

Psalm 23:4

So do not fear, for I am with you; do not be dismayed, for I am your God. I will strengthen you and help you; I will uphold you with my righteous right hand.

Isaiah 41:10

Train a child in the way he should go, and when he is old he will not turn from it.

Proverbs 22:6

That if you confess with your mouth, "Jesus is Lord," and believe in your heart that God raised him from the dead, you will be saved.

Romans 10:9

Flee the evil desires of youth, and pursue righteousness, faith, love and peace, along with those who call on the Lord out of a pure heart.

2 Timothy 2:22

But how is it to your credit if you receive a beating for doing wrong and endure it? But if you suffer for doing good and you endure it, this is commendable before God. To this you were called, because Christ suffered for you, leaving an example, that you should follow in his steps. He committed no sin, and no deceit was found in His mouth. When they hurled their insults at Him, he did not retaliate; when he suffered, he made no threats. Instead, he entrusted himself to him who judges justly.

1 Peter 2:20-23

But you will receive power when the Holy Spirit comes on you; and you will be my witnesses in Jerusalem, and in all Judea and Samaria, and to the ends of the earth.

Acts 1:8

For this God is our God for ever and ever; he will be our guide even to the end.

> Psalm 48:14

Therefore, get rid of all moral filth and the evil that is so prevalent and humbly accept the word planted in you, which can save you.

> James 1:21

Be perfect, therefore, as your Heavenly Father is perfect.

> Matthew 5:48

In the beginning was the Word, and the Word was with God, and the Word was God.

> John 1:1

So whether you eat or drink or whatever you do, do it for the glory of God.

> 1 Corinthians 10:31

Before I formed you in the womb I knew you, before you were born I set you apart; I appointed you as a prophet to the nations.

> Jeremiah 1:5

Dear friends, do not believe every spirit, but test the spirits to see whether they are from God, because many false prophets have gone out into the world.

> 1 John 4:1

Jesus answered, "I am the way and the truth and the life. No one comes to the Father except through me."

John 14:6

Therefore go and make disciples of all nations, baptizing them in the name of the Father and of the Son and of the Holy Spirit.

Matthew 28:19

Do not conform any longer to the patterns of this world, but be transformed by the renewing of your mind. Then you will be able to test and approve that God's will is – good, pleasing and perfect will.

Romans 12:2

And I will do whatever you ask in my name, so that the Son may bring glory to the Father.

John 14:13

This is the confidence we have in approaching God: that if we ask anything according to His will, he hears us.

1 John 5:14

"For I know the plans I have for you," declares the Lord, "plans to prosper you and not to harm you, plans to give you hope and a future."

Jeremiah 29:11

Let everything that has breath praise the Lord. Praise the Lord.

Psalm 150:6

For the wages of sin is death, but the gift of God is eternal life in Christ Jesus our Lord.

Romans 6:23

...And surely I am with you always, to the very end of the age.

> Matthew 28:20

Nevertheless, I will bring health and healing to it; I will heal my people and will let them enjoy abundant peace and security.

> Jeremiah 33:6

who forgives all your sins and heals all your diseases.

> Psalm 103:3

For you, O Lord, have delivered my soul from death, my eyes from tears, my feet from stumbling.

> Psalm 116:8

A cheerful heart is good medicine, but a crushed spirit dries up the bones.

> Proverbs 17:22

Remain in me, as I also remain in you. No branch can bear fruit by itself; it must remain in the vine. Neither can you bear fruit unless you remain in me. 'I am the vine; you are the branches. If you remain in me and I in you, you will bear much fruit; apart from me you can do nothing

> John 15:4-5

The Lord God said, it is not good for man to be alone; I will make a helper suitable for him.

> Genesis 2:18

For God so loved the world that He gave his one and only Son, that whoever believes in him shall not perish but have eternal life.

> John 3:16

Love the Lord your God with all your heart and with all your soul and with all your strength.

> Deuteronomy 6:5

Children obey your parents in the Lord, for this is right.

> Ephesians 6:1

Now as the church submits to Christ, so also wives should submit to their husbands in everything. Husbands, love your wives, just as Christ loved the church and gave himself up for her.

> Ephesians 5:24-25

Greater love has no one than this: to lay down one's life for one's friends. You are my friends if you do what I command. I no longer call you servants because a servant does not know his master's business. Instead I have called you friends, for everything that I learned from my Father I have made known to you.

> John 15:13-15

May the grace of the Lord Jesus Christ, and the love of God,
and the fellowship of the Holy Spirit be with you all.

2 Corinthians 13:14 NIV

www.ingramcontent.com/pod-product-compliance
Lightning Source LLC
Chambersburg PA
CBHW020020050426
42450CB00005B/571